My Emotions

Written by Chemise Taylor

Illustrated by Alexis B. Taylor

Copyright © 2020 by My Skills Books

Published by My Skills Books

All rights reserved. No part of this publication may be reproduced, distributed, or transmitted in any form or by any means, including photocopying, recording, or other electronic or mechanical methods, without the prior written permission of the publisher, except in the case of brief quotations embodied in critical reviews and certain other noncommercial uses permitted by copyright law.

First Printing, 2019.

ISBN: 978-1-951573-13-3

www.myskillsbooks.com

She feels happy.

I feel happy, when I am having fun.
When I feel happy....

- I can say, "I feel happy!"
- I can do fun things I enjoy.
- I can ask someone to come and play with me.

She feels sad.

I may cry or want to be left alone when I feel sad. When I feel sad....

- I can tell someone that I feel sad and why I feel sad.
- I can ask an adult for help.
- I can do things that I enjoy or spend time with friends.

He feels scared.

I feel scared when I don't feel safe.
When I feel scared...

- I can tell someone I am scared.
- I can ask an adult for help.
- I can find a safe place to go.

He feels mad.

I feel mad, when something I don't want to happen occurs. When I feel mad....

- I may scream or yell. I may say or do hurtful things.
- I can ask an adult for help.
- I can say, "I feel mad." and why I feel mad.

He feels tired.

I feel tired when I do not get enough sleep at night. I may feel tired after jumping, running and sometimes after playing. When I feel tired...

- I can say, "I feel tired."
- I can take a nap.
- I can sit down and rest.

He feels surprised.

I feel surprised when something unexpected occurs. When I feel surprised....

- I can say "I am surprised."
- I can ask an adult for help.
- I can ask questions about what is going on.

He feels sick.

When I am sick, I may cough, sneeze or even throw up. When I feel sick....

- I can say "I feel sick."
- I can ask an adult for help.
- I may need to see a doctor, take medicine and/or rest.

She feels suspicious.

I feel suspicious, if I am not sure of what I am seeing or hearing. When I feel suspicious....

- I can ask for more information.
- I can ask, "Is that real?" or "Is this true?"
- I can ask an adult for help.

He feels curious.

I feel curious, when I see or hear something unfamiliar. When I feel curious....

- I can ask for more information.
- I can ask an adult for help.
- I can gather more information on my own.

Book Details

Story Word Count: 385

Key Words: Happy, Sad, Scared, Mad, Tired, Surprised, Sick, Suspicious and Curious

Comprehension Check

- What was the story about?
- Name 3 emotions?
- What can you do if you feel sick?

Reading Award

This certificate goes to:

_____

for reading "My Emotions"

Good Job!

More books, apps and resources at myskillsbooks.com

www.ingramcontent.com/pod-product-compliance
Lightning Source LLC
Chambersburg PA
CBHW042110090526
44592CB00004B/77